Thriving Entrepreneur

Kathy Kidd, Monica Reed, Ann Gamble, Connie Knudson, Dionne Garvin, Noreen Henry, Rodney Lawson, Steve Kidd

Copyright 2017 Kathy Kidd. All rights reserved. No part of this book can be reproduced in any form without the written permission of the author and its publisher.

Contents

Forward 7

What Will You Do With Your
Opportunity? 11

Passing It On 17

The Headline of Your Life is Success ... 24

My Journey from Parallel-preneur
Towards Entrepreneur 33

Prospering in Life 39

Say Yes to Your Next Step 49

The Feng Shui of Personal
Transformation From Depressed & Stuck
to Financial Abundance 56

Just Show Up 68

Forward

by Jennifer Kem

Entrepreneurship is the most courageous choice someone can make. It requires grit and grace, heart and hustle, and testing and failing and succeeding. Most of all, it requires resilience and living intentionally every day. Easier said than done? Yes. Worth it? YES.

For almost 20 years I've worked with entrepreneurs and celebrities, personal brands and Fortune 500 companies and you know what? The thing that they're seeking to create is no different than your own. At the end of the day, all businesses have to be clear on who they are, answer why prospective clients should care, and be consistent and persistent...every day.

If that sounds exhausting or overwhelming, I'd offer that you may have some work to do on the inspiration and motivation side of the equation. The truth is that people don't know who you are, until you help them.

One way to take that first step (and then many, many more after that), is to tell our stories, and bridge them to our customers' stories. This means taking what they desire and mapping a path for them to walk towards us. But too many times, we think our stories aren't "sexy" enough or "deep" enough. Let me be one of the first to (or one of many who've already) tell you, that your story matters.

A thriving entrepreneur is a rite of passage from being ignited by our stories and dreams, to stumbling into the spinning web of all the tools, frameworks, books and teachers available in this noisy world, to finding the courage to putting ourselves out there to hopefully getting our first sale. All of these things aren't linear - in fact, many of the steps to become a thriving entrepreneur have everything to do less with the blueprints you follow and more to do with how you manage the journey between your ears and the walk in your talk.

Let me explain a little further.

Many of us draw Inspiration from the stories that have driven us to take the courageous path of the entrepreneur. But to stay in the game, surrounding yourself with like-minded, authentic people who will lovingly yet firmly help you stand in your truth in a noisy world is what true Motivation comes from.

That's what makes this anthology from Kathy Kidd, highlighting the real stories of fellow entrepreneurs, such an asset for you. You're obviously reading these words right now, and so you want to be inspired and motivated, right? The good news, you're going to get your fill of that inside the following pages.

But it doesn't stop with motivation, or even with the telling of your story. It starts with 3 important things that will help you build a business and a brand with an advantage more than anyone else:

1. Do something imperfectly every day. You want to train the muscle of doing so you can establish yourself as an expert or resource as much as possible. If you focus on perfection, you're wasting time not helping someone who needs to hear your message now.
2. Be around like-minded people. Join a community that is comprised of people who are helpful, knowledgeable and generous (and be the mirror of that as well). There are groups and forums online that are perfect for this - even if you're an introvert. To grow a thriving business, you need other people.
3. Tell your story consistently and persistently. This is a noisy world, and social media is not going away. Let your story be the nucleus of what continues to inspire and motivate you even when the going gets tough. Re-

member that your story was the most likely catalyst of why you wanted to start a business in the first place.

Most of all, I hope you see that your story and celebrating the stories of your customers is the bedrock of a brand that gets seen, heard and paid. In Thriving Entrepreneur, I hope you are inspired and motivated to be near others who are on the journey with you. Step into their shoes, see their path (including the rocks and valleys and hills they've walked to get here), and then boldly go forth with building your dreams with the tools they share with you. Let's go.

Jennifer Kem
Founder, Master Brand Method

What Will You Do With Your Opportunity?

By: Kathy Kidd

My life today is barely recognizable. It's perfect by no means, but I have many blessings to be thankful for. As I look over the last few years, I've had the opportunity to travel to elegant locations and speak on stages alongside some of the world's greatest minds and leaders. I've masterminded with Fortune 500 entrepreneurs. What I appreciate most of all, is that I have the freedom of choice. I can choose where I want to live. I can choose how I want to live. And, best of all are the choices I can offer my children. This is a long way from where I started.

In my mid-twenties, I was at a very low point. I had PTSD and anxiety disorder with agoraphobia. At one point, I couldn't even leave the house for three months to so much as check the mail. Things were pretty bleak and as I looked at my future, I wondered if I could just have a "normal life". I knew that at the very least I needed to survive and I had the hope of a bright future. I always had the entrepreneurial spirit and with the internet being the up and coming thing, I thought "What if I could do something online, from home?"

I was in a really, really, tough spot. Needless to say, I had a very limited budget. My mom was kind enough to buy me a computer for Christmas. I was so grateful for that used 486 PC (before Pentium chip) and the most basic dial up internet connection. It was hope and connection.

I got ahold of book on basic HTML and I started teaching myself how to do web design. With that little computer and book, I made my first website in March of 1997. I caught on pretty quickly and was able to start making websites for other people and actually made an income from home. I was able to grow my business, get better and get healthier and support myself. A few years later, I met my husband, Steve, through a mutual client. We merged our businesses into one company. We've been working to build a successful company, together, for more than 15 years.

I've always believed in the American dream that

you can be and have anything you choose, if you're just willing to do what it takes. With the power of the internet, and computers at our fingertips, more people than ever have access to that dream! Around the world, across our nation, no matter where you live, if you can get an internet connection, you have access to all of it. If you can take the bus to the library, if you have a computer at school, if you put a computer in your home, or even if you have a cell phone at your fingertips with access to the internet, you have access to build your own version of the "American dream". Being globally minded, it's really so much bigger than anything we've ever had available to us.

It reminds me of so many success stories that I've seen over the years. Let me share just a few with you. One of my favorites was a woman who lived out in the middle of the desert, surrounded by tumbleweeds. She had a computer with internet access and she was trying out building an online store. She made test products, using pictures of something that she had a lot of around her—tumbleweeds. Surprisingly, somebody found those tumbleweeds and wanted to buy them. So, she started making her first sales and all she was doing was testing it out! Pretty soon it was Hollywood film set designers buying tumbleweeds. Then, a clothing designer needed some for a photo-shoot. She became a very successful business owner selling tumbleweeds. Who would have guessed there was need for such a thing?

You may have seen Ree Drummond on the Food Network, or her kitchen products in retail stores. However, she didn't start there. I first met her in our homeschool moms group, about 15 years ago. I remember when she started her blog. She posted on various topics of the daily life for a rancher's wife and homeschool mom, but the recipes quickly became the most popular. The number one thing I can say about Ree's blog, watching it grow and evolve over the years, is that she posted consistently. Now, you see her throwing down with Bobby Flay, or on her own cooking show, Pioneer Woman.

Both of these women started with nothing more than a computer with internet connection, and lived a far distance from the nearest small town. With the internet at their fingertips, they had access to learning, opportunity and potential clients around the world! You do, too.

Imagine if they had never taken that leap! Imagine if they never even bothered to try. Imagine if they let their self-doubt stop them from taking the next step. Where would they be now? Also, imagine if they had done it just a little sooner.

So, I want to challenge you to chase your dreams. What can you do to take one step, today? What opportunities do you have at your fingertips? Your dream is within reach. Just start. Layout three simple steps for yourself.

Your three simple steps might look something like this:

Internet access on a scheduled basis. Whether it's in your home or you have to take a bus to the library, schedule that time and make it important.

Choose the type of internet based business you want.

Take action: get training, a business license, start a website, whatever that next step is for you.

Get those three things done. Then evaluate what your next steps are. Begin to make progress today, because the opportunity is there, now! The internet gives you the opportunity to reach, not just the community that you're in, but anywhere around the world. You're no longer limited to just the people next door. So, whether you have a niche market or something that will feed the world, you have access to a whole wide variety of potential clients. Just take that first step.

.

Kathy Kidd
KIDDmarketing.com
BestSellersGuild.com

Passing It On

By Ancleah Gamble

Throughout the course of my life, I've been involved in several businesses. Reflecting back to my earliest childhood memories, I realize I get this incredible entrepreneurial drive from my dad. My father has always been successful in business. What began as what some may call a 'side hustle', quickly grew to a sustainable, thriving business. No matter the position he held professionally, there was always that business he had on the side. Whether it was the computer consulting business in the 80's, or his wildly successful insurance agency, I know I learned my work ethic from him. My father was my model of success, and honestly, he still is for my brother and me to this day.

What I learned from him more than anything else, is that you must define what success is for you. In order to thrive as an entrepreneur, you have to live YOUR version of success. And to do that, you need to find out what success looks like for you. You shouldn't make that determination based off of someone else's vision. You have a million times over to be the best you, or you can fail a thousand times mimicking someone else's success. I've learned someone else's success won't be as fulfilling. When you define and go after that thing for yourself, only then will you truly thrive.

For me, my definition of success has always been to have time with my children. Quality time with my children was my vision of success and pushed me to thrive as an entrepreneur. I needed my business to be successful so that I could create quality moments they would remember for a lifetime. One of the things I did to accomplish this was to create a business with my children. The idea was birthed watching them. I kept seeing food unexplainably disappear from my kitchen pantry. I kept wondering why the variety bag of chips or the box of snack cakes would be completely empty in less than 24 hours. I knew they weren't eating them all in a day. I discovered they were selling them to their friends. I wanted to hone whatever was driving them and harness it into a business that was beneficial to us all. This business would accomplish a few things. First, working together would create that quality time with them I yearned for. Second, I knew they would learn the work ethic I learned from my father. And the third thing, which happened to be a bonus, my children would potentially earn enough to help with their quickly approaching college years. Considering they were in their pre and early teens, I wanted to turn up the heat on the 'paying for college' conversations we've been having since they began grade school.

I wanted my children to participate in paying for college so that I could help to instill the same work ethic and sense of community as my parents did with my brother and me. I didn't want my children to just expect that they were going to get student loans, or that I would shake the magical money tree and it would rain thousands of dollars on their heads. No, I wanted them to actively participate in their success, through working hard to obtain scholarships or through hard work earning extra money. We talked proactively and we came up with a way to help fund part of their education.

We created a food truck business selling shaved ice. To begin with, we just directed our attention on small community events, going around in neighborhoods and showing up at little league games. As the business continued, it grew to the point where we found ourselves at large city events. The larger events really gave us exposure and helped us to actually make pretty good profits. So much so, that we were not only profitable, but we were profitable enough to be able to donate a percentage of our earnings to the charity, or the organization that was hosting the event. This allowed me the ability to show my children what it meant to not only be an entrepreneur, but to also be a contributing member of our community. I learned this from my mother. My first and best example to this day of a servant's heart is my mother. Growing up, my brother and I were always reminded by our mom that we should not walk through life with our hands out but make sure we look for opportunities to positively contribute to society. That message stuck with me and I have passed on my personal mantra of 'living is giving' to my children. So I wasn't surprised that my children were enthusiastic about donating a percentage of our proceeds from a hard day's work to each event thereafter.

As the business grew, our knowledge grew; we learned more and more, and my teens became that much more involved in the success of the business. I was amazed at their ideas to grow the business and their efforts to better serve our customers. We changed our business model from just selling shaved ice to also include some light food items. We discovered that slight change allowed us the ability to increase our revenues by over 120%.

My teens learned that they could create a business plan. They learned customer service skills, and from the experience with running a business, they discovered a joy inside of themselves that comes from really doing something that could be enjoyable and profitable.

As the teens began to graduate, we all took a vote, because I knew that I wasn't going to be able to continue the food truck after they were gone. We voted to sell the business. The best part about that is, the proceeds from the sale of the truck also helped them to pay for part of their education.

The business was good for me. I got to spend fun, yet hard working moments with my children. We created quality memories that will last a lifetime. This was my vision in action, my vision of a success. I love that I was not only teaching them invaluable business skills but I was also passing on a legacy. I was passing on the legacy of work ethic from my father and that of a servant's heart from my mother. Again, remember, for me, success was being able to spend time with my children. By doing so, I was not only teaching them business and passing on the legacy of my parents, but we were also spending time together and they were actually enjoying being entrepreneurs. It was good for them. It was good for me. And another unexpected bonus is that we were able to make a product that allowed us to donate to worthwhile events and charities that needed help.

What I learned was that it is never too early to teach your children the fundamentals of life and business and how to really do what you all love and thrive. If I had an opportunity to do it over, I would have started even sooner. I'm confident they would have wanted to do the same and we would have likely experienced even more success.

I believe that our children have a propensity to be entrepreneurs if we are available to nurture and encourage them through the process. Two of my children, now that they are grown and in college, are working on building their own companies. Another has just begun to look at entrepreneurship. So, out of four, three of them now are working on being entrepreneurs themselves. They have learned through experience that hard work can be rewarding and have begun to define what it means to them to be successful.

I want you to know that you have a voice, for you and for your family. You can make a difference. You can thrive. Don't give energy or thought to anything contrary to your vision of success. Tune out the doubts. I'm here to tell you that when you take that leap of faith, even if it is a somewhat scared leap, it will be worth the energy and the effort. Get out of your own way and move from the fear of failure or the fear of success and just take the leap.

Small intentional steps taken every day move you that much closer to your vision of success as a thriving entrepreneur.

You can find the joy, the success, and the real ability to thrive as an entrepreneur when you create and do the thing that YOU define as YOUR vision of success. Stick with it; be persistent, even through the obstacles. The reward will be worthwhile. Don't let anyone or anything deter you. Begin to create meaningful connections with the right people; build a supportive tribe. By finding that supportive team and doing that thing that really makes you thrive, you too can live as a thriving entrepreneur.

Ancleah Gamble
Endless Business Management
www.endlessbm.com

The Headline of Your Life is Success

By Rodney Lawson

No matter what we set out to accomplish in life, being an entrepreneur, a parent, or to work our way up the corporate world's ladder, the headline is success vs. failure. Everything we do with our lives, all we want from it, is success. Just think, no one really wakes in the morning and says, "My goal is to fail at every damn thing today!" Therefore, in order to really thrive in your life or in business, you need the headline, the goal, the ultimate end of what you're setting out to accomplish; it needs to drive you feverishly towards success.

Now that we know success is something we as human beings thrive for, we must look at another intriguing factor; how is success defined? True success lies within the eyes of the beholder. For some it's financial inclines, for others it could be advancing their education. Some folks even define it as developing their kids; instilling positive values and virtues. Even if it's subliminal, every person has a prioritized list of what outlines success and that sits within their core values. There are so many things that come into play with success, but for the sake of brevity we will discuss how it pertains to that of a thriving entrepreneur. It really boils down to a few basic principles:

1. Ensuring your success stay within your core values
2. Fulfillment in success comes by doing what you love
3. Creating a culture you can be proud of

Now, let me go more into detail providing specific examples of the importance for the two factors.

First, it's living your life or doing something that you're able to maintain. Ask yourself, "Is this something that works within my value system? Is it something I get internal personal satisfaction with or does it feels like work?" Here's a very personal yet clear example.

As a leadership executive, I was hired as a general manager heading up an operations facility. Upon taking the job I was told the performance and the personnel were one of the worst in the company. My goal, my charge, my measurement of success lay with two factors:

1. Turning the environment around to one of ultimate performance through inspiring the workers.

2. Upward movement or advancement within my career for a job well done.

Through instilling accountability measures, developing the staff, and ensuring they were positively motivated; something I coined "The 33 and 1/3 Rule", I had the office performing at approximately 73% higher than they were before I took over. You might think, "Wow, that's success!" Yes, it was massive success but the problem is, it only touched my 1st measurement of success not the 2nd. I still defined my success as advancement in the company as well as turning the office environment around into one of positive production. The problem with the second measurement of success is there was a senior leader whose character was unbecoming and extremely unprofessional in his actions. While my boss reported to him, I wanted absolutely nothing to do with him. Not only did he treat people like they were beneath him, his narcissistic ways were so far removed of how my values were wired. I knew that by not 'playing ball', a term used when one in the corporate level is unwilling to go along with the group, it would result in me having an extremely dismal chance of being promoted. I didn't' care! I would not waiver on my values. Yet most importantly, I didn't want group association to take over in having folks assume I was like that of him or one of his surrogates.

Fortunately, as we were taken over by another company, our CEO came in saying he didn't care for 'workplace bullies'. Needless to say, the executive with the extreme case of narcissism was let go within the first week of the acquisition.

You see, although I defined success in my own terms, I was not willing to go against my core values for what I deem a successful outcome. It wasn't a difficult thought process for me either. My values come before any success I strive for and I can live with that at every turn.

In every situation one must weigh their options and move forward with that which they can live with when it comes to success. This also exemplifies the importance of knowing your core values as you thrive for success as an entrepreneur.

To my second point, is the success fulfilling? Specifically, when you're talking about being an entrepreneur, is it going to be fulfilling work for you? We all have a lot of ideas. Sometimes we're blessed to be able to figure them out quickly, but sometimes we struggle with it. Some people find that, although the idea of being an entrepreneur was really appealing in the beginning, after getting into the thick of it, they quickly learn that it's not what they thought. Ultimately to thrive, you need to set the concept of thriving in your life ahead of thriving as an entrepreneur. Only through living and doing what you love will place you in the life that you're meant to live, the life that you define as successful, only then can you begin to really achieve success at a high level.

In addition, there are so many little things when it comes to business that you need to also watch. Is your product good? Do you take good care of your customers? How is your strategy working? In the end, it is really important to look for that gratifying feeling. If you're not 'getting a high' off of taking care of people then it's difficult to achieve success in a people-centric arena.

For me, I've spent all of my adult life in relatively structured environments. Having started in corporate, way back at 18, the structure feels good to me. I know what to do inside that environment. I know, if I found something procedurally incorrect within the company, whatever the challenge, that it would be something that I could learn from. I knew that both, in the business that I was working for, as well as a business I wanted to create. I knew I would do something different if it had a negative impact on me.

In order to see what's good and what's bad and to learn what to do and what not to do in business; I look back on all the businesses and corporations that I've worked for and I see the parts that I enjoyed. I then look at the parts that I didn't enjoy. It's not that I really like structure, but that I know when I put it in place with my life, I'd have the freedom to create the path to build upon my success, and to live in a place of joy because without it, I would stumble.

I remember 15 to 20 years ago, interviewing for a job. As part of the interview process, they sent me to go see a psychiatrist. He said to me at the end of it, that my profile showed me to be someone who, at some point, was going to go off and do their own thing. Now, at the time, it didn't seem real, but I found that it was very true. He told me that some people can be okay just doing side projects, but many people with my personality type know that they have to go out and become full time entrepreneurs. He was right and it was a while going from there to where I am now, but it did happen.

I remember when I started out and decided I was going to move towards that direction. I was building a speaking career and only 10 to 20 percent of my time would go towards building my business. Well, over the years that same 20 percent had grown to the place where it was more like 70 to 80 percent. My frustration in the corporate world, or should I say my love for creating my own brand, culture, and product, guided me, and for a little while I actually went without a corporate job.

I was given a great piece of advice and that's not to burn up your runway, not to eat up all the capital that you have. I was told my investment dollars were like sand flowing through an hourglass that would eventually go away if I didn't replenish it. Instead I was told to seek out an investor, a place I could work to pay my living expenses and provide for my business until it could sustain itself. Once I get to that point, I would have my success and my freedom that I was seeking as a thriving entrepreneur. By embracing the concept of having an investor in my life, rather than running out of money, I am now accomplishing both tasks—saving and using what comes from that investor to supplement the growth of my business.

We all have challenges as we thrive for success. What I believe in is actually part of thriving, and that is to see those challenges and then be able to overcome them. One of my fun challenges is deciding on which area to tackle first since I've created countless content over the years working in the business world.

I have the opportunity to make money coaching people, writing, speaking, doing management development for corporations, and even doing presentations at universities. It's a very wide, diverse range of projects. So, the challenge at this point in my journey as a thriving entrepreneur is, what do I focus on? Of course, I want to do it all.

It all comes from the core of me knowing, at my heart, all I really want to do is serve other people.

In conclusion, my final point and advice is to thrive in your own life and business creating your own organizational culture. No matter where you are in that process, you have to develop the culture of you, that is, the kind of person that you want displayed to the world. If you don't create it yourself, the world and the people around you will dictate that to you. Many folks make this mistake focusing solely on talent; yet failing to understand the image projected to the world, to their customers, colleagues, or friends.

As you establish this deep culture character, it will guide you in a direction for life and help you with understanding what path to take when faced with life's challenges. As I reflect, even way back when I was still in corporate full-time, I had not created a business of my own at this juncture but I knew what

I wanted. I decided that for the corporation of Rodney Lawson, LLC, I was going to develop what I wanted for my image and what I wanted for my character in the world. From this thought, my brand is clear and the culture has been established completely into the company I now have and run today.

Remember, you create the character. You create the culture of your company. By doing that, you can live as a thriving entrepreneur to find that success and have the headline for your life be success.

Rodney Lawson
Rodney Lawson LLC
RodneyLawson.com

My Journey from Parallel-preneur Towards Entrepreneur

Noreen N. Henry

There is always hope. For me, living as a thriving entrepreneur, more than anything else, has to do with living life on my terms and knowing that in the midst of things, when things seem their worst, peace, joy, and happiness are ours. We can live in that place of peace, joy, and happiness on a daily basis, and always having hope.

I have a goal to be an entrepreneur coaching, speaking, and training. I love the thought of the freedom it will give me, to have more time for my family, to spend my time doing what I want to do when I want to do it, in helping others, and creating a non-profit organization to help the youth. Doing these are fulfilling for me. As Lisa Nichols says, when good people have money, they do more good in the world.

Right now, I'm working as a parallel-preneur, and upon retirement from my day job, I will transition to a full-time entrepreneur. The best part about my life now though, why I can say that I'm thriving as an entrepreneur, is because I have peace. I am complete. I now have a great focal point. I know what I want to do with my life, and I know where the Lord is leading me. For me, more than anything else, that is what it means to be thriving.

I've always known I wanted to be an entrepreneur. I did different things over the years with network marketing ventures, but it wasn't until, about a couple of years ago, that I got the focus I have now, truly knowing what I really want to do that is fulfilling to me. Most of what I did before weren't exactly me, or allowed me to be completely focused and happy in what I was doing. Now I have that focus, now I know what I want to do and what I'm truly passionate about, I can live every day of my life as a thriving entrepreneur helping people to have positive lives regardless of the negativity around them.

Practically my whole life, I've helped others as they were going through issues in their own lives. I help people through by teaching them the tools that will help them to stay in joy, peace, and happiness to overcome in their situations to victory, but more than that, to be loving and compassionate to them. It's what I'm truly passionate about. Now, we all go through life issues, and there is help to get us through that I'm happy teaching about. I love to see people's lives changed for the better with my help, and that is thriving entrepreneurially for me.

Over the years, I've taken counseling, coaching, speaking, business classes, etc. in preparation of being an entrepreneur. In doing these classes, it has helped focus me to now know and really understand what I enjoy doing. Finding that true purpose has helped to transform my life for the better even more so.

Knowing the Lord's direction in our lives is what helps us go through to become the overcomers that we are meant to be. Sometimes there are things that happen in our lives that are difficult that we need to overcome, and I want you to understand that, in the end, they will turn around for the good as we use the tools that I teach and with my coaching, etc.

Just like me, you can find that thing you are going through to be the thing that turns around and you can help others with it. It is possible to live every day in peace, joy, and happiness, I can attest to that. I didn't realize earlier on in my life how much I could overcome, that it was possible to live in peace, joy, and happiness every day. There was a time in my life when going to work, things were difficult and were a struggle because I didn't have the tools I have now. But now, when times are tough at work, with the knowledge I've gained over the years, I have peace, joy and happiness regardless of what is going on.

It wasn't that long ago that one of my children, as they were transitioning to adulthood, really came against me. They were just being mean to me. It was very tough, but what I know is, through all of it, I had peace. I was able to keep praying and even in that difficult time, I kept that peace, and I didn't make it worse by feeding into it as I would have done years before I had the tools I have now. I simply stood on the scriptures and the promises of God, that told me it would be okay and that God was in control, and I was able to live in that place of peace, joy, and happiness, even though it was real challenging at times.

People would say to me, I don't know how you are doing it, I couldn't be so strong. As I look back at it and reflect, things are so different now. I will always remember that it was the Lord brought me through the very tough times.

As parents, we raise our children. We want them to be the best version of themselves. Then, sometimes they do have moments like my child had where we look at it and we're like, what is going on? But, you too, can stay in happiness, live in peace and joy.

You will overcome. You can live in the struggles until you do overcome. It will be tough, it isn't necessarily easy, but as you focus on the peace, you can work through it and find victory in the end.

In order to start learning to live victoriously, the first thing you need to do is step back and look at the situation and analyze what is really going on. Then create a strategy of how you're going to get from where you are to where you want to be. First of all, of course, pray about it and ask the Lord to lead you through it.

One example is my job. There have been times where I could have gone to work sad, discouraged, and without hope; but I have focused understanding of what the Lord is leading me to, I use the tools I learned over the years to overcome, and I have peace knowing that I will get through it. I want that understanding and help for you too.

Rather than going to work depressed or going through other issues in your life being unhappy and down about it, know that there are promises from the Lord to help you and get you through the issues by standing on His promises. That is the strategy that you need to create for yourself, and that is what will help you get through to victory. By simply finding the promises for what you are going through, will help you to you go through where you will overcome and have breakthrough in the end.

And, during the midst of your trials and tribulations, because you have a strategy, because you're constantly trying and knowing there is a way to overcome, you can live each day in the midst of it and be at peace, joy, and happiness. You know, without a doubt, that things are going to work out no matter how bad things look. That's how you can live as a thriving entrepreneur, because you will know that, no matter what is going on, God is in control, and there is always hope. I'm living proof of it.

Noreen N. Henry,
Overcomer
Coach, Speaker, Trainer
Victorious Living Culture LLC
noreennhenry@gmail.com
https://noreennhenry.lpages.co/victorious-living-culture/

Living Your Most Authentic Life

by: Dionne Garvin

I believe that all of us have the desire to prosper. My definition of the word prosper, is to find and use purpose to make a positive impact on the hearts and minds of others. I never ran into anybody that doesn't want to prosper, and to do it just being their most authentic self.

Discovering our most authentic self is a dynamic, ongoing journey. Most people think it's a one-time occurrence – you find your authentic self, and that's it, you've arrived. You can check personal development off on your to-do list. Yet, there are aspects of our "authenticity" that morph and shift through time and our experiences. There are core parts of us that always remain the heart of who we are, but the morphing and shifting happen as life happens – things like career changes, parents aging, marriages, children, and other societal evolutions – are what cause us to have to go back and reinvent what being our best and most authentic self may mean at different points in time in our lives.

My authenticity is a huge part of my atypical entrepreneurial story: I work for an outstanding multinational corporation, and I love the work that I do. I also run a thriving small business and lifestyle brand, The Expressionista. I am deeply passionate about my corporate work, and about our mission to support young, ambitious women at The Expressionista. This IS my most authentic life as a thriving entrepreneur.

I love pouring in the lives of the women that I serve, and helping them to prosper by cultivating their most authentic life. What I found is that the more you nourish the people you serve, your ability to nourish increases, and you are able to serve more and more. I liken it to one of my favorite stories in the bible, a townswoman has a limited number of jars and oil in her home, and the prophet tells her to start pouring the oil. The more oil she poured, the more she had to pour. Giving and serving in that way becomes a cycle, an incredible energy that grows with each life changed from experiencing YOU. There is no better way to live and thrive as an entrepreneur than to find yourself surrounded by people that you've helped to nourish and seeing them soar.

My belief is that we thrive as our most authentic selves when our lives are centered around three key things: love, people, and purpose. All three are foundational needs and desires that we are born with, and help us to know and live in the heart of our most authentic life. As a mindset mentor, a purpose catalyst, and a confidence coach with a mission to help ambitious women live authentically, I believe that a woman centered in love, people, and purpose becomes an unstoppable force, a powerful voice to those that she serves, and, in turn, she has the power to change the world.

The Expressionista was birthed out of the recognition of a void for young ambitious women that sought to make their mark on the world, but felt like something was missing. They were told to lean in, know your worth, don't settle, be bold and fearless. While those messages were incredibly inspiring, they didn't provide instruction, and left many young women feeling lost and alone after the moment of inspiration wore off. After getting back to her day-to-day life, often she ended up giving up and settling for the status quo, which silenced her voice, and in turn prevented her from touching the lives and hearts of many. I watched this happen over and over again with so many women. And I knew the pattern so well because I'd experienced it myself.

And for me, it was during a few life shifts and changes that purpose and my voice dimmed. I was disillusioned, exhausted, and overwhelmed – and I was unsure of where to turn. With the fear of failing slowly creeping in to my purview, I felt like I had only one choice to help resolve all of the frustration, angst, and petrifying fear that I felt.

And that choice was to hide.

If I hid, I could avoid questions, appearing as if I didn't know, and breaking down in to a pile of tears from the pressure to constantly appear powerfully, even though I was drowning in feelings of uncertainty and fearing the unknown. And then, I discovered, I wasn't alone. I started talking to other women that were experiencing the same things, and needed the support to live courageously, to be reminded to love themselves and to operate from the deepest place of love within their hearts; to connect with people powerfully and intentionally; and to pursue purpose with passion and conviction. And to share the beauty of their authenticity while doing it.

And I love helping women become the best version of themselves. In our programs, we see women truly transform from silent and hiding to powerhouse leaders, using their voices to empower themselves and others. Our tools help that woman who has experienced those inspirational moments, but needs some supports to begin discovering and living in her purpose just what she needs to accomplish her life' s work. The results are astounding. We have seen woman speak up and easily gain promotions and raises; receive television interview and spots; create community organizations created to serve and transform underrepresented populations; families created and sometimes reconstructed to be stronger and more resilient; we see relationships restored and rebuilt.

This year, I was working with a client from one of my signature programs, called Purpose, Promise and Poise. She's now a private coaching client but in that particular moment, she was a participant in our group program that helps women find their purpose and align their mindset. She shared her recent personal experiences around her life, career, relationships, and community work with the group. While I was listening to this wonderful young woman, I could tell that what she really needed was to just hear someone tell her that she was going in the right direction. That she was growing. She truly was developing into the person that she wanted to be and the person that she always seen herself becoming. I sensed that she really needed to be reaffirmed, that although she wasn't straight out asking for it, I connected with her and heard her "questions" behind her stories. What she was really asking be sharing was, "Am I doing this life thing right? Am I doing what's best for me? Is this what is most purposeful for me? Am I serving in a way that makes a difference?" Have you ever found yourself thinking and feeling that way?

Now, I can't just tell my clients their right direction as a coach. That is something that each of us has to decide and figure out for ourselves. You have to have your own life direction, because if I were to tell you where you're supposed to go, you would be living my life direction for you and not your own true purpose.

I remember her saying specifically; I know I'm looking for answers. Do you think I really have this answer in me? I mean is it something that I really can know? Is there really only one way? And if there is one way, what is it?

She's not alone. SO many of us are asking those same questions when we seek advice from friends, a parent or relative, a mentor, a coach, or even the internet. The truth is, there isn't really one way, but there is a best way. The way to discover YOUR best way is to begin trusting what's already inside of you. Listen to that still, small voice that speaks from the center of your soul, talk to God and receive guidance from Him or if you believe in another wisdom tradition, seek the process for connecting with the higher power of your tradition. Then make a sound decision and go for it.

As we discussed feedback with her, I immediately began to see a shift in her. I saw her move from that place of uncertainty to a place of inner trust and reliance on what she already knew to be true. See, that's it - you can answer your biggest questions better than anyone else when you stand in the power of your own connection. That connection is a connection of love and of purpose. That connection is a wellspring that helps you thrive. By looking at what's already inside of you, you can stand in your own tremendous power and purpose, and impact the lives of the people around you.

So, I'm sure by now you're asking, how do I do this? You see all that you want for your life, can be yours. How? Start by getting clear on where you are today. First, start by examining your mindset. Do you often feel positive and encouraged and see great things happening for yourself? Do you feel defeated and as if you shouldn't believe the best because it may "set you up to fail"? Second, think about what you give to the world, that no one else can give in the way that you do. That is purpose. Do you know and understand our purpose? What place do we have in our life, in this world? Last, think about your relationships. What is your connection to the people in your life? List them out, and list what's happening in those relationships currently. Do you see a pattern between these three? If you're honest with yourself in your reflection, you will see one emerge. And sometimes you can't see it – and that's why we're here to help.

We help our clients to discover the alignment between their mindset, purpose, and connections, and identify what's working and what may be holding them back from living at their best. I believe that spending the time to do this is one of the highest forms of self love. It connects you with YOU, so that you can connect more wholeheartedly with your purpose, and with people.

As we examine who we are and how we desire to grow, we can start by making simple tweaks, for example, in the way we think. With my private clients, I walk them through the Mindset Maven™ program and framework to help them examine their core beliefs, identify hindrances, and to create a set of powerful thoughts that move them in the direction of their desires. Mindset Maven is one of our primary offerings because I strongly believe that in order to thrive, our minds have to be focused on the right direction.

After our mindset is in place, then we really do need to clearly understand our purpose. In our Purpose, Promise, and Poise workshops and group coaching sessions, we use a methodology called the Declare Method, which helps you to identify your Desire, Emotions, Capability, Likability, Afflictions, Rules, and, Experience. Putting all of those together, I have seen women discover and begin living in their purpose quickly – because it's such a simple approach that gives significant clarity quickly and comfortably.

Simply taking these pieces and putting them together, you can identify the path you need to get on as well as identifying the changes and the things that you may need to transform in your life in order to get to where you know you're meant to be.

I've been honored many times and continue to be honored to help people get to that "ah-ha moment" where clarity comes in and they discover how to cultivate their most authentic life. I think of one of my private coaching clients that I recently worked with that discovered a part of her purpose was centered in teaching. At her core, she was a teacher. All that she did revolved around the act of teaching – but her approach was not traditional, and classroom. It was experiential, and centered on activities for teen girls and young women, and helping them develop a healthy self-esteem. She discovered through our sessions that she needed to create her own non-profit that supported girls and women to build healthy self-esteem and to develop healthy, lasting relationships. Now, to see her share her incredible wisdom and open heart with teens and women is amazing. The blessing is that it also expands my heart and mind. Both in person as well as online, it fills me with joy to watch and realize, as you and all the others that I want to live as thriving entrepreneurs, move into living authentically, with purpose, and in a way that helps you prosper in life.

Dionne Garvin
www.expressionista.co/contact/
letsgo@purposepromisepoise.com

Say Yes to Your Next Step

By Monica Reed

A thriving entrepreneur is simply someone who knows their purpose in life and is willing to live out that purpose. It is someone who is not willing to stop until they have succeeded. Every one of us is made with a purpose, with a reason why we're here. Often, as we grow up, go through schooling, go out into the working world, we lose our sense of what that true purpose is. Rather than living fulfilling lives, we find ourselves working a job and trying to advance in a career. Many times, we either don't recognize, or we stop one day and do realize that we're not feeling fulfilled. We're not living in the center of our purpose and without that, our lives, our marriages, and everything around us just doesn't seem to work quite right. As a new entrepreneur, I've been struggling with the new lifestyle yet loving it all at the same time because now I get to live in my purpose.

I remember two years ago, the questions at work begin to come at me. Maybe you've had those kinds of questions at work too. Where you're sitting there, doing your job, and you're saying to yourself, what is my purpose? Why am I here? For me, I was working for a legal corporation. Planning events, and volunteering for different organizations while bringing people together was an after-hour passion for me. While hosting events and workshops, I didn't really realize that what I was doing at the time was basically entrepreneurial. When I really stopped, and looked at the things that I wanted to be busy with, I came to see that my passion was being distracted by the corporate world. I loved doing things that brought people together and the opportunities to encourage others. The only time I enjoyed being at work, were the times that I was on break planning events or talking to my clients and assisting them with the things that brought them joy.

"Then why are you sitting here doing something that does not bring you joy?" was a constant question in the back of my mind.

My next thought was "God then show me what I need to do in order to be truly fulfilled."

I remember saying to myself, "Monica, you will not be able to hear what God is trying to tell and show you if you continue to live within the noise." I was constantly available to everyone else, however I would press the hold button when it came to my own life and dreams.

As I've been working my way through and learning how to be a thriving entrepreneur I had a real eye opening moment. It had to be about a year ago in my journey. I used to collect legal documents for a company. It wasn't until I received my own legal documents, which happened to be a garnishment across my desk, when I kind of realized that the whole corporate system was not set up in a way to help me support my family and there was something wrong with it. Here I was being served a garnishment working for a company and making someone else a millionaire and they weren't even paying me a salary that would not even allow me to pay for the garnishment that I had received. Somehow, it just didn't seem right.

I'm not going to say it was upside down or backwards, but I started to realize that the corporate world wasn't really what I wanted.

After much contemplation, I discovered that, for me, in order to truly thrive in life, I needed to remove the distraction of the corporation world. That was the moment I knew that I had to focus and really live out what I'm here for. To make the difference that I'm meant to make in the world, I left corporate. Now, of course, I had to have a discussion about my decision with my family because it did have some monetary impact on our lives. I was nervous about the changes that my children would have to endure. I struggled with thoughts that I was being selfish. I had struggled with the thought of my children struggling. I also struggled with the thought that my life would have wait until they were out of the home. Then I realized that my children were already suffering from a lack of a full potential life because the corporate world had determined my worth. Was I scared? Absolutely! Did I know what to expect next? No. However, I couldn't afford to not know what possibly could have been waiting for me. So, *I did it!*

Scared but determined, I jumped, afraid, and left the corporate world.

With that last piece of information, I made that somewhat scary leap into the unknown but also, into my purpose. I spent time initially, after I left corporate, really honing in on what I was meant to do. Looking back at all of the jobs I had because, let's be honest, none of them were really careers that I was invested in. They were work that I was doing simply to just make money. I saw that the string amongst all of them was the people that I was able to serve, the relationships that I helped to build.

I remember people coming to me and asking me questions about their relationship and I was able to help and answer them. Then I knew what my purpose was. I became a relationship coach. I didn't even know before then that it existed. It was so true to the heart of the passion that I had in life that I knew it was something that I not only could do, but I would love doing. That is for me, what it really means to thrive as an entrepreneur. Now I get to help couples connect and to encourage them during their personal challenges. I also get to show them tools that they can use to strengthen their marriage.

Everyday my life gets to be about teaching and helping people and seeing great results. Whether it be in person, at events, or in workshops. I'm helping couples know that they can overcome the challenges they're facing. My husband and I have been together for 22 years and we've been through issues of our own. We've had to work our way through it. I feel blessed because of the place that we've come to, that I can help other people.

For example, a couple that I worked with, who were in the process of getting a divorce, had been together for almost the same amount of time as my husband and I had. As I began to talk to them, I realized that the problem, more than anything, was that they needed a reset in their mindset. As we talked through their life, we began to let it all emerge. We talked about all that they had come through, and we continued to talk through that concept of the mindset around our marriage.

It's so easy to let one thing go bad and cascade into a whole ton of problems, but as they began to see that they could remove the negative, they had the ability to overpower the past. They could look past the problems that seemed so insurmountable and begin to build positive experiences and thoughts. It helped them realize how much they were missing in their marriage as well as to be able to get rid of a lot of things that they had been holding on to. One of the things this particular couple realized was the outside influences in their marriage were creating within them a mindset that was pulling them apart. I'm so delighted to be able to celebrate with them that they were able to keep their marriage together. And that, in a nutshell, is what it means for me to live as a thriving entrepreneur. To identify what your life's purpose is.

It's not about focusing on the money. But, rather focusing on where you can serve others. If you really put the service of others at the forefront of your mind, everything else begins to fall in place. Rather than being, like so many of us have been, where we go to work every day and we spend every day unhappy. Instead, you find that inner focus and happiness and truly live in your purpose.

As an entrepreneur, we get the opportunity every day to serve our clients with the things that are the true purpose of our life and I know from experience how exciting that is. I know that you will find that as you serve others, your life will be exciting too. Live your life to the fullest of your purpose. After you discover what your purpose is, then strive for your dream. I encourage you to say yes to your next step because your next step may just be your BEST step!

That's how we can live as a thriving entrepreneur.

Monica Reed
Mymarriagematterstoo@gmail.com
www.MrsMonicaReed.com

The Feng Shui of Personal Transformation
From Depressed & Stuck to Financial Abundance

by Connie Knudson

How a Child Care Teacher Became a Feng Shui Consultant

I am a Feng Shui Consultant. I live in a beautiful apartment with a beautiful view and I work with a wonderful Feng Shui Master, the world-renowned Marie Diamond, who has transformed the lives of people around the globe with her amazing *Diamond Feng Shui* strategies. Because of Marie, I have learned to look deeply at your home, office and personal energy to give accurate and beneficial guidance for maximum results. She does both space and time Feng Shui, which gives you a way to "stack the deck in your favor." It's based on quantum physics and the ancient wisdom of the Chinese Masters. I make it easy for you to achieve the results you wish to attract. With the dynamic element of time Feng Shui, along with space Feng Shui, my clients get amazing results when they take my advice to heart.

But it wasn't always this way. Two years ago, I was working at a corporate job, working long hours, and not making enough money to pay for the healthy food that my body required. I am very frugal because of my upbringing, and back then, even more so. I remember one day I was in line to pay for my groceries, and I saw that the total was more than what my weekly budget allowed, so I said, "Put the cherries back." I wanted to stay within my weekly budget, so I didn't mind. A kind woman in the line behind me said, "I'll pay for it. Keep it." I was embarrassed that someone had over-heard me. I said no, but she insisted. So I just took it that the Universe had my back and that my lesson was to learn to trust that I am supported by the Universe.

Prior to that incident, had lived for six years teaching Kindergarten in Honduras, and when I returned to the United States, my teaching job was gone. I had to start from scratch. I had a Master's Degree in Early Childhood Education, and the teacher certification to work with kindergarten and elementary children. But when I returned from Honduras, the educational system no longer wanted me. My friends were encouraging me to try again and go on interviews, but in my heart of hearts, I knew that I was destined for something bigger and better. This just wasn't my path any more.

Out of fear, and a need to earn money to pay my bills, I got a job as a "teacher" in a Child Care Center. It was heart-wrenching for me. I had been trained to work with Kindergarten and primary school children, but it's very different from working with children ages 2 - 4, and specifically teaching them reading and math skills. I felt like my heart was breaking because I wanted to spend time with each child individually and give them the time and attention they deserved, but that's not the skill that the job required. This was child care, not education. I have a gentle voice and the loud voices of the other teachers seemed to me more like yelling. They were able to command the attention of the group, but not touch their hearts.

I wanted to advocate for a kinder, gentler approach, and better nutrition for the children. But I was not in a position to say anything without endangering my job. My job was to comply, make the children obey, and follow the rules. I felt helpless because nobody around me saw anything wrong with the food. In that environment, nobody understood the nature of the child, as I had understood from my Montessori training. It was a constant battle within myself, to keep my mouth shut and the frustration inside of me continued to build. I became depressed and desperate to get out of this situation, but I saw no way out.

Einstein has said that no problem can be solved in the same energy that it was created, so in order to move forward, I had to change my energy. I had to find something to like about the job, in order to prevent a continual downward spiral. So I hired a business coach to help me raise my mindset and begin to build a health coaching business. With her kind support, I was able to gradually create a pathway out of this "stuckness." I learned how to give talks in the community and market myself. My big lesson was to find something positive about every situation, and to be grateful for those moments of joy. I prayed and took baby steps in the art of meditation, to help me stay positive. I worked on my book during my lunch hour and I looked for places to give talks after work. These were my baby steps. I learned about the Law of Attraction and started doing positive affirmations to re-train my brain.

Even though I was improving my mindset, I still wasn't making the progress I needed to, to make a big breakthrough. I just knew I was destined for something bigger. Sometimes it's time to take baby steps, and sometimes it's time to get out of the environment that didn't resonate with me. I knew that I needed to take bigger action. HUGE action. I had to leave the Child Care industry because my heart was exploding, demanding to be heard, desiring to make a difference in my own life, and in the world. So a couple months later, I was able to take that huge action. Here's how it happened.

Feng Shui Lifted me out of Depression
One day in desperation, I decided to ask the advice of a Feng Shui teacher I had heard about in El Paso. I couldn't afford to pay an actual consultation, but this kind man recommended a book, written by his teacher. I got the book at Barnes and Noble and started reading to get an understanding of how Feng Shui works.

I moved things around in my home. I moved my bed. I set some goals, and wrote them out on little cards. I started placing images and items around my home to reflect my goals. When I started doing these things, my depression lifted almost immediately. One day, I saw on the Internet a beautiful and well-known Feng Shui consultant being interviewed. I was mesmerized by what she was saying, and I heard how people were able to transform their lives in dramatic ways and increase their financial abundance. I knew in my heart that it was true, if only I could put into practice the principles she described. I wanted to learn everything I could about Diamond Feng Shui. I listened to the recording over and over, to get inspired and get a better understanding. I signed up for a Diamond Feng Shui Course to get the guidance I needed. I placed her picture on my

Vision Board, with the goal of meeting her in person, so that I could absorb and learn even more. I have kept it there ever since, and today, she is my Teacher and my Mentor.] I have learned so much from her, and today, my life today is completely transformed from the way it was just two short years ago.

I work on myself and my Feng Shui every day, and the more I observe, the more I see how the images around me have influenced the way I live and the way I feel about myself. I can see that the Universe has my back, and that the right people have come into my life at the right time, even more so with the right images and surroundings. In the beginning, I took baby steps. I listened to and read everything I could about Diamond Feng Shui, which delves into the dynamic energy of time, as well as space Feng Shui. It is based on quantum physics and mathematical formulas, which Marie has spelled out in simple, easy-to-follow steps. She delved deep into the knowledge and wisdom of the ancient Feng Shui masters, and has made it easy for the modern mind to understand. This is something I love helping people with, because I know it worked for me, and it can work for you, too.

Feng Shui and Life Transformation

Two months after starting my Feng Shui journey, I made the decision that I needed to move to a different, more supportive environment, where I could grow my business, grow personally, and attract the right healer for my health challenges. Because of my Feng Shui and my mindset, I was able to retire, pack up my home, and move to a new and exciting place for me: Albuquerque, New Mexico. It felt full of promise, for creating health and better opportunities to build a business.

As I prepared to take the important step of retiring, I never saw it as a rest, but rather opening up opportunities to grow create a venue for my dreams to come true. I was able to find an online job teaching English that allowed me to support myself as I built my business from scratch and started to make connections with new people.

When I moved to Albuquerque, things didn't change overnight. I rented a room in a home, and started teaching online, and focused more intensely on building my business. It felt so good, not having to go anywhere to earn money. Instead I was helping children on the other side of the globe, to learn to read, write and speak English.

A year and a half after I retired and moved to Albuquerque, I was able to move into my own space: a Cooperative Living apartment. I re-read my goal card that I had written a year earlier. It said: "I now live in a beautiful apartment with a beautiful view." That's where I live. BINGO! Yes, my Feng Shui was working. I checked my bank account, and I noticed that almost two years after retiring, my income had greatly increased, and I had more than enough for my needs, with enough to invest in my business.

Feng Shui isn't magic, but it often feels like it. It has freed up the energy in my environment to inspire my mind with ideas that are leading me to my true destiny in this life.

Feng Shui and Health—the biggest transformation of all

Since the age of 11, I have been dealing with severe asthma. Sometimes up, sometimes down, and always searching for the cause and the solution. This is why I became a health coach, and this is how I have finally found some tools that work.

During my lifetime, I have searched high and low and tried hundreds of approaches, supplements, herbs and healers to help myself. Some things work, some don't—but the only reason things don't work is because I hadn't found the cause, and therefore the solution. But this year, 2017, it got worse than ever before. All I could do was breathe. The meds were no longer working. I was taking my nebulizer and having to take it more & more frequently. When I had to take it every 20 minutes, I knew it was time to get help NOW. So I went to an Urgent Care Center one more time.

I activated my health direction and then sought medical help. Coincidentally, I heard words of guidance from my teacher, who said to look for allergies. To be honest, I didn't like that advice because I'd already been there, done that and it didn't work. But this time it was different. I felt that she saw something in me at an intuitive level, and I took action on her words of advice. I started looking for a natural allergy healer here in Albuquerque, and I found one.

Though the previous 2 years I'd tried different healers in Albuquerque, this time I found what I was looking for. This one brought me results that stayed with me, and I found some of the causes. After the first allergy treatment, my wheezing stopped. This was after one week earlier, I had landed in an Urgent Care center with extreme difficulty breathing. My nebulizer was no longer working. I barely made it down to my car to drive myself to the Clinic. My oxygen level was ten degrees below normal. My temperature was low. Even with this serious a situation, my treatment worked.

It has been 2 months since that first treatment and my breathing continues to improve. But that's not where the story ends. After the allergy healer, I found another healer who does the same kind of treatment, combined with energetic healing of the body, mind and spirit. At this point, my life continues to improve on many levels. If you ask me, I'd say that I got my life back. I can say that this transformation is what makes my life so worthwhile now. I am so grateful! Feng Shui helps open up the channels to attract the right person, the right supplement or the right partner into your life, when you use it in combination with spiritual practices such as meditation and personal affirmations.

Create an Abundant life with Feng Shui
Inspired by Marie Diamond's courses and personal advice, I have been able to create the kind of life that I love, and I'm still expanding and growing. I tripled my income in two years. I implement Diamond Feng Shui to the best of my ability and continue to learn more, as I observe my results.

That first year, I had placed Marie's photo in my success direction on the Vision Board that I created. A year and a half later, I decided to do Feng Shui as a business and take my success to the next level. About a week later, I received a phone call from Marie Diamond herself. She called ME on the phone. I was so excited and encouraged by that. I will never forget the moment that I heard her beautiful voice saying, "Hello, this is Marie Diamond."

I now work from home and have an increasing number of clients who want to work with me. When they hear about the kind of Feng Shui that I do, which includes both space and the dynamic energy of time, they want to discover the endless possibilities for themselves.

People hire me to help them with their business or their home, because they want to increase the flow of financial abundance. Others want to improve their health or the health of a family member. Feng Shui works at a deep level. It's based on the science of quantum physics, combined with the wisdom of the ancient Chinese Feng Shui Masters. I am so blessed to be guided by the knowledge and wisdom of Marie Diamond. Because my knowledge is on a solid foundation, my clients get very good results.

It all started by taking baby steps. What about you? Are you ready for greater financial abundance or transformation in your life? Go to my site www.connieknudson.com to find out how we can work together to boost the abundance in your business and your life. I look forward to meeting you!

Love & Light,

Connie Knudson
https://www.facebook.com/Connie-Knudson-Feng-ShuiAbundance-1172876349461471/

Find me on Facebook to find out how we can work together to boost the abundance in your business and your life. I look forward to meeting you.

Just Show Up

by Steve Kidd

As the host of Thriving Entrepreneur, more than anything I am always overwhelmed at the opportunity to bring the show and all of my guests to you each week! I am so grateful every time I step in front of the mic to know you're listening. It's such an honor that you would allow me to be part of your life on, hopefully, a weekly basis. We have such amazing guests. Our Best Selling Authors, as well as some amazing world changing entrepreneurs that come on the show. And I love sharing them with you. With each author I do hope that you run out and you get their books and you really take in the things that they're putting out there in the world. It's such an amazing thing to see what each of us has in us to put out into the world.

From all of our staff here at KIDD Marketing, I can tell you it is so cool for us as we learn and grow from what each of our guests and clients share. We know, as we have helped people develop, we have also been blessed and grown. More than anything I just really wanted to make sure that you all really know how appreciated you are by both Kathy and I for your contribution to the little thing that we try to do in the world by helping people share their brilliance with the world. And, while you're writing a book, why not make a bestseller, right? For me being part of these amazing people's journey is what it means to be a Thriving Entrepreneur.

Being a thriving entrepreneur, comes in so many different packages. I love the intro to my show, Mark Pogue's music is awesome, but I also love it because it says right up front that I've been blessed to be the son of a minister, the grandson of a minister, and to work in the ministry myself, both in and out of the church. I love in life and business all of the different ways that we can be of service. In the last 30 years what I do for people in business has been called things like: mentoring, training, leadership development, business coaching and many others. All which boil down to helping people get to the next level in their life and their business. It is a blessing to see them grow and bless the world with their gifts.

For me, what it means to be a thriving entrepreneur really doesn't have to do with whether or not what you do is a full time primary revenue source, or simply just an expression of being what you are meant to be in the world... I think the difference between being a thriving entrepreneur and just being, Joe Employee, really has more to do with the amount of yourself that you put out into the world. Whether that be through a corporation or even a 9 to 5 blue-collar kind of a job or as a full-time business owner, doesn't matter. It's about not being the kind of person who is just allowing life to take them wherever with no goal and no purpose. Really, truly, thriving entrepreneurs, no matter where they work, whether they've been an entrepreneur for years, or are just an amazing employee, are the kind of people who their passion shows up every day in what they do. They don't allow a day to go by without living it passionately and allowing the best pieces of themselves to really come through in what they do—to show up—and that's probably the best explanation I can use, is to really truly show up, is what it means to be a thriving entrepreneur.

If you will invest the time, if you simply take the time to do what you do wholeheartedly, your ability and your passion make a difference that only you can make in the world. I recently saw an episode of Shark Tank on TV where the lady owned a $50 million dollar company and still worked her fulltime job as an optometrist because of the passion she has for optometry. That, to me, was just the perfect example of living as a thriving entrepreneur because the place that she makes her money, the thing that she needs to put out into the world, and her particular job title can all be different things. Thriving is all about maximizing all of who you are.

Sometimes, for some of us, our passion and our job coincide completely. Some entrepreneurs are absolutely are 100% fulltime from can-to-can't, being an entrepreneur. And, for others, the way they earn their money and how they express their passion are different. For you, that's really the key. It isn't how many hours you put in, it isn't how much you identify yourself as being an entrepreneur, it's about showing up. Can you show up in your life? I look around and it's interesting because I'm fifty years old and so, there are times, when like an average, older gentleman, I will find myself saying things about these younger kids, and sometimes I even laugh, sometimes I'll look at Kathy and I'll be like, you know I sound like an old guy don't I? But the truth of the matter is that no matter what generation you want to look at, baby boomers, generation X, or a millennial it's not about what other people think about you, it's about you really showing up.

I've been blessed to experience some millennials that are totally just outpacing the millennial bad rap. They're like, "No, I may have been born between this date and that date, but that's not what defines me. What defines me is the passion that I have in the world and how I show up. I want to show up, show out, and show the world what it means to thrive" and, to me, that really is the heart and soul of being a thriving entrepreneur.

There are people who work in church and, as their fulltime job, both ministers and laypeople, that I absolutely know are thriving entrepreneurs. Sometimes as a minister, you have to be very savvy in business in order to help your church make it. But again the business side of things does not define them. Showing up where they are needed and living passionately, doing that thing that only they can do. As I'm always saying on the show, you are uniquely brilliant. You were created for a purpose in the world, absolutely the world needs you. That is what it means to be a thriving entrepreneur, is when our purpose and our passion get together with us just simply showing up and doing that thing that only we can do.

When each of us shows up in the fullness of our passion, and our purpose and we use all of our ability, in that thing that we're meant to do, when we really show up in that manner, the world is a better place. If you want to look for the answer, in my opinion, to just about any situation that you see going wrong in the world, it really boils down to every single person showing up in their unique brilliance. The world is a better place when each of us really lives out their purpose.

I don't know if you've ever been to, a restaurant, or a store, where a person just really shines. Where they're thriving in the position they are in is evident. Just being around people like that can make you feel better. I can't see a better way to show up as a thriving entrepreneur than to affect and impact the people who come in contact with you. To me, that really does live out the thing that I say at the end of every episode. "Kathy and I are here to help you live every day of your life as a thriving entrepreneur." We really do want that for you. And I hope that in your purpose and in your passion, you are thriving. I hope that in everything, you do you show up. I know that if you will show up, you will live as a thriving entrepreneur.

Steve Kidd
KIDDMarketing.com
BestSellersGuild.com

www.ingramcontent.com/pod-product-compliance
Lightning Source LLC
Chambersburg PA
CBHW050015230526
45470CB00003B/972